A PAGAN BOOK OF HOLIDAYS
Children's Poems for Prayer and Practice

J. C. Artemisia

Copyright © 2017 J. C. Artemisia

All rights reserved.

ISBN-10: 1974610829
ISBN-13: 978-1974610822

DEDICATION

To my children, Brogan, Trystan, and Oliver. You have truly shown me blessings come in threes.
May magick hold you, guide you, and show you the beauty in every moment.
I love you always.

CONTENTS

	Acknowledgments	i
	Introduction	1
1	Yule	2
2	Imbolgc	8
3	Ostara	14
4	Beltane	20
5	Midsummer	26
6	Lammas	32
7	Mabon	38
8	Samhain	44
9	My Family Traditions	50

ACKNOWLEDGMENTS

A special thanks to my husband—for your confidence, encouragement, and partnership.
Thank you to Ophelia, my guide and companion.
Many thanks to Jenn Monroe—for your support with this work, your passionate instruction, and your inspiring mentorship.
And of course, perpetual gratitude to the Gods, Goddesses, and mystic spirits in your various forms.

INTRODUCTION

In these pages, you will find rhyme, lore, prayer, and nature to fill your Pagan holidays with more love and more magick. I hope these stories find a home in your celebrations.

At the end of the book, you will find a section to write or draw about your own family traditions. Continue to grow in kindness and love, and celebrate the blessings all around us.

Blessed be,
J.C. Artemisia

YULE

Cold-lace spirals onto glass panes
catching hot breath exhaled
in bellyfuls of air that stain
the window with a veil.
Outside, the shivering winds blow,
howling for a friend
to play beneath the falling snow,
to build a man and pretend
that he is real. And though his eyes
are buttons, and his arms
are fallen twigs, his grinning guise
of happiness will charm.

Today, the sun is special;
today, the sun is new,
and in the sky where he will dwell
there is a blue-gray hue.
The Holly and the Oak Kings
will have a battle grand,
and now, on through the warming spring
the Oak King rules the land.
Together with the newborn sun,
he'll thaw the frozen ground,
and when their work is rightly done
bright flowers will be found.

We sleep too long by accident;
the new sun rises late.
The sky's still dim, though morning's spent;
his light is not yet great.
We follow him throughout the day,
as through the clouds he peers.
They slowly cover him in gray,
and then he reappears.
His stay is brief within the sky;
the night will soon close in.
Tomorrow gives another try,
as his long year begins.

As we embrace a brand new year
under a brand new sun,
all but good thoughts will disappear
as happiness is won.
Exhale, as sadness slips away;
breathe in, accept the light.
Rejoice, as strength grows in the day,
and sleep soundly at night.
The season next will hold for you
much possibility;
as long as goals are followed through
success is guaranteed.

We sit down with our paper pads,
our pencils and our pens,
recalling all the good times had
with family and friends.
We write down all our hopes and dreams
and place them on our trees
with branches still so evergreen
despite the winter freeze.
Our tree glows with colors of spring;
it's sturdy, and it's strong.
So, through the seasons it will bring
our wishes right along.

At Yule, under a sun so bright,
may you be blessed by all his light.

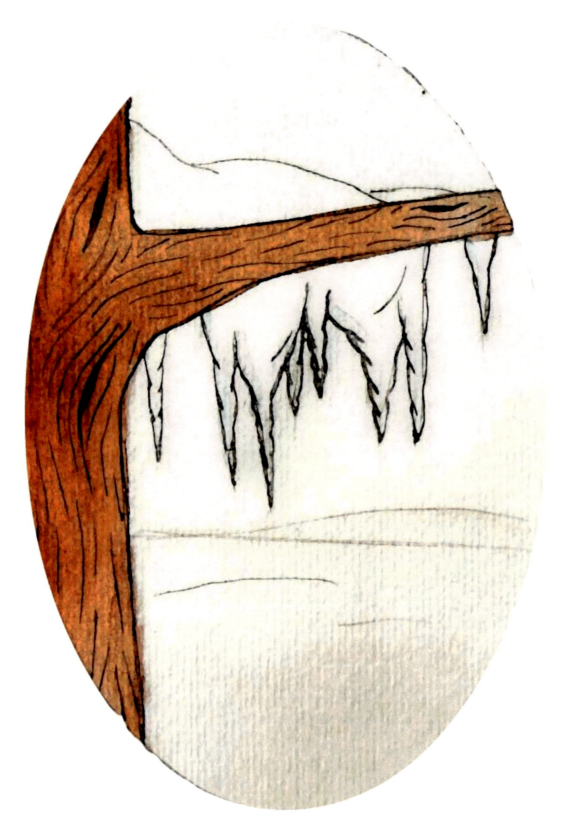

IMBOLGC

Snow birds are quiet as they plot
their move to cooler air.
They'll fly away when days grow hot
and snowflakes become rare.
Thunder-gray skies are glittered
with golden dust at noon,
and though the wind remains bitter,
the sun lessens the gloom.
At night the icy cold returns
and winter winds hover;
we stay inside where we have learned
to bundle under covers.

In milk, they rest, mother and child,
under a sky so dim.
She sings songs in a voice so mild;
her love is all for him.
She gives him milk so clean and white,
and he grows strong each hour.
But still they sleep, in longer nights
reserving daytime power.
Her touch for him is always sweet,
so he'll be gently learned;
her softness makes the sky complete,
as into spring we turn.

The frozen branches start to sway
their icy finger tips.
This warming ice will melt away
as winter loses grip.
The Lady makes the earth revived;
the new, young sun will aid,
and when the springtime has arrived,
we'll have our clean slate made.
We thank her for her healing touch;
brown grasses will turn green.
Already, she has done so much
to warm this winter scene.

It seems we've spent a lengthy time
with white earth at our feet,
and now we wish for shades of lime
and flowers smelling sweet.
We pray for color in the fields
and for new birds to sing.
We wonder what the earth will yield
as we move into spring.
We hope this year will grow the same
as many years before;
so at Midsummer's final flame
we'll harvest it once more.

We bring our milk outside and sit
under a big oak tree;
our Lady's praised by pouring it
into a creamy sea.
Onto the roots it splashes then
it seeps into the mud;
the puddle foams a little when
the earth absorbs the flood.
Before the Lady we all bow,
and to her little one;
to keep her honor, we do vow,
and then our prayer is done.

*At Imbolgc, sweet as her caress,
sleep well, and know you're rightly blessed.*

OSTARA

On the distant blue-gray hilltops
white snowcaps still remain,
and drips from icicles still drop
beyond the window panes.
Outside the air smells like the thaw,
like thick and leafy greens,
and birds, returning, start to caw,
another signal gleaned.
Soon, all the animals will come,
out from their winter sleeping,
and fuzzy friends will run about
all chittering and squeaking.

The baby sun from Yule has grown
and now will share his smile.
He lights the morning sky alone
and stays there for a while.
We see his light is now stronger;
he shines it from above.
As daytime spreads ever-longer
he radiates his love.
Today, he's strong enough to help
the little flowers grow,
he turns the soil and warms it well;
he'll melt away the snow.

The flower petals, so brand new,
grin brightly at clear skies;
they sparkle with the morning dew
that glitters at our eyes.
Today, the earth becomes so clean,
despite the puddled mud,
and lime stalk grasses grow as green
as every flower bud.
It's good to feel the warming sun
instead of winter's cold,
and spring has only just begun
to bring forth new from old.

Some eggs can hold life like a seed,
and in the spring they hatch.
When colors from the ground are freed,
we paint our eggs to match.
Yellow like the marigold,
blue like violet heads,
so many colors to behold
like pansies, pink and red.
Sometimes, we hide our eggs outside
and play a finding game;
just like a flower's bloom—*surprise*—
we discover them the same.

It's never wrong to make mistakes;
it happens to us all.
But making up is what it takes
to let ourselves stand tall.
The spring will teach us to be kind
to family and to friends.
It cleans our hearts and clears our minds
to make a good amends.
So, take time to apologize
for mistakes that you have made
and peace of mind will be your prize
as due respect is paid.

*Ostara's blessings unto you
will be found in green fields of new.*

BELTANE

The sun has brought the flowers up;
    their colors are so bright.
Violets, mums, and buttercups,
    create a splendorous sight.
His rays are warm and fill us, too,
    with happy-colored thoughts.
We sparkle like the morning dew
    at all that he has wrought.
We lay in shade that he creates
    through leaf and flower trees;
all day, we stay and simply wait
    to taste another breeze.

At night the sun's warmth still remains;
    it warms us to our core.
And even in the late spring rain,
    our jackets, we ignore.
We dance in summer-kissed raindrops
    and stomp bare feet in mud;
yet, even when the raining stops,
    the dance stays in our blood.
His warmth is now a part of us,
    even as dusk grows near.
The fire glow tells us we're blessed
    and that we've none to fear.

A blaze to be his finest hour—
the sun's passion descends,
and blushes color to each flower,
and glitters dew-drop gems.
The daytime's getting longer still;
the hot sun burns like fire,
and for his heat he knows we will
continue to admire.
We gather in the shade he casts
through treetops full of leaves;
we nap in shadows, warm and vast—
another gift received.

A rainbow braid is tied as we
string in and out and play,
and once it's woven we will see
what we've made for this day.
The maypole draws together all
the colors of the spring,
which decorate the pole so tall
as families dance and sing.
We appreciate the splendor
made here for all of us,
and together we will render
a symbol that is blessed.

Always with our moms and dads,
we light the Beltane fire.
Shared memories will make us glad
around flames, which inspire.
Patchouli incense for the sun,
on this his special day,
is burned until the light is gone
and daylight fades to gray.
The ash, we save for later on,
which our Sun God has blessed.
Its power is strongest at the dawn
when sunlight's had its rest.

*The sun brings all the colors close
and loves all, not just one the most.*

MIDSUMMER

Today is bright in sun and air
as morning fills the sky
even before the roosters blare
can wake us up from night.
Shadows are scarce and hide away
underneath rocks and stones,
as brightness floods the earth today
in yellow-golden tones.
His warmth is like a giant hug;
it's how we know he cares
about all things—from big to bugs—
he hears all of our prayers.

When nighttime finally falls, today,
the hour is very late,
and prayers are made in an array
to kings in battle great.
The darkness dulls out all the gold;
the air becomes so still.
The leaves on trees will inward fold,
planning for winter's chill.
Dewdrops formed on the evening's grass
glisten under the moon,
glittering in fields like mirror glass
now ready to attune.

This battle is waged twice a year
the battle of the kings,
and at Midsummer time we cheer
the King of Holly wins.
With just one touch the leaves will turn
to orange, brown, and red.
White snow replaces fires burned
as over earth it spreads.
The Holly King in his dark cape
will sit upon the throne,
and from the cold we won't escape
until a new sun's grown.

Wooden tables are gathered round
under the glorious sun.
Singing and laughter are the sounds
of families having fun.
We feast on cool, fresh, summer treats
delicious as they are:
watermelon and whipped cream sweets
and cookies shaped like stars.
Outside, we all enjoy the day
with merry company,
sharing smiles as we all play
in summer gayety.

The grapefruit sun slowly descends
into the vast skyline.
The longest day of this year ends
as sunlight dulls in shine.
We stand here all remembering
the months filled with warm light,
but now under the Holly King
that green will turn to white.
The days are shorter from now on;
the nights grow still and deep.
The new king spreads the darkness long
to soothe the earth to sleep.

Though sun fades from Midsummer's sky,
his love and warmth will never die.

LAMMAS

We're ambling through sweet meadows;
tall stalks of wheat grass sway.
Fruits and vegetables still grow,
but they're not ripe today.
The sun rises in salmon skies;
the scenery is beige,
and grasses, once bright green, disguise
themselves in pallid sage.
The breeze is stronger than it was
when summer first had come.
The sun recedes as winter draws;
the warmth is almost gone.

Lugh has hushed the sky with reason
since the horned kings' fight.
He lights the sky for crop season
as winter takes the night.
He makes a present of his love,
the love his queen gave him,
and lets the final rains above
fall onto each tree limb.
The joining of the rain to land
will help the harvest grow,
and like the joining of two hands,
hard work will always show.

Today, we celebrate King Lugh
and his bountiful queen.
For them we sing, *hip-hip hurrah,*
upon a Lammas scene.
They bless us with our stalks of wheat,
that stand so thin and tall,
the crop that makes the wind smell sweet;
we know it's almost fall.
We thank them for the love they share
and harvests yet to come,
which bring us close to show we care;
our spirits join as one.

Bread tastes so good with sweet jelly;
it makes our mouths say, *yum!*
It satisfies a loud belly,
but where does bread come from?
Well, first its wheat, in many rows,
those long and slender stalks;
it's harvested from where it grows
and brought to bakers' blocks.
Ground wheat makes dough,
and then is raised;
its warm scent floats on air.
When done, the rolls and loaves amaze
with bounty we can share.

At Lammas-time we slice the bread
our friends and families bake.
With butter or with fruity spread,
we grab our loaves to break.
There's bitter herb, with salty crust,
some seed, dark wheat, and rye,
sweet swirls of cinnamon—we *must*
have one small piece to try.
Companion means 'with bread and friends.'
Togetherness is fun!
And though our celebration ends,
harvest is just begun.

*We rise together like the dough,
and as a family we will grow.*

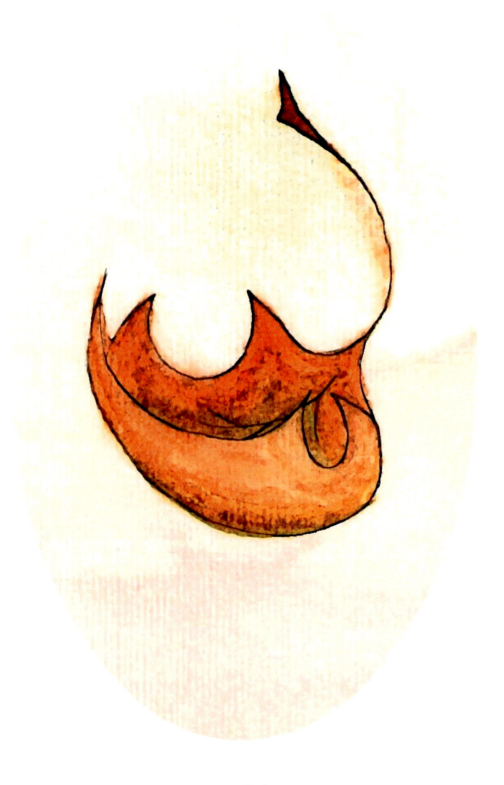

MABON

The wind is cool, it whips and swirls
around and through the trees,
and aging leaves will fold and curl,
defeated by the breeze.
The edging of each leaf becomes
a tiny work of art,
as green changes to red and plum
from out— to middle part.
The grasses turn to sandy brown;
the frost will soon appear.
The leaves will all come tumbling down.
Hooray! The autumn's here!

The tabletops are filled to brims
with freshly hand-picked fruits,
and vegetables do well to trim
in salads and in soups.
There's apple crisp, and apple pie,
and apple cider, too.
There's berry juice we have to try—
our family's secret brew.
The vegetables are popped or steamed
or simply eaten cold.
A harvest feast that could be dreamed
is wondrous to behold.

They first were blossoms on the trees,
just tiny, little flowers,
which grew to fruits with help from bees
and from sweet summer showers.
With basket, box, or bag in hand,
the croppers make their way,
to reap the sugars of the land
we celebrate, today.
They'll gather apples, peaches, grapes,
for juices and for pies.
They'll gather fruit of any shape
then hurry home their prize.

In patches and on vines and stalks
the vegetables all grow,
and so much fun it is to walk
through golden, cornfield rows.
Their smell is faint, but oh, so sweet;
their crunch is cool and clean,
and some will hold a tasty treat
inside their husks so lean.
We lightly fill the sides of plates
with carrots, peas, and beans,
for nothing makes a meal so great,
as fresh and crispy greens.

Willpower is a strength inside
that keeps us going on.
It shows the most when we have *tried*,
not just when we have won.
In fields when fruits are picked away
and veggie harvest's past,
the farmers must remember they
have more to harvest last.
Their work continues through Samhain;
they work because they must,
until the harvest moon does wane
and soil turns to dust.

*We're blessed by sweetness all around
and give thanks before leaves are browned.*

SAMHAIN

So many candles light the sky
where stars cannot, through winds,
which draw them back to where they shy—
peeking through branches thin.
The early moon will smile through
an avocado haze
then cast her light upon the blue
backdrop of night, for praise.
Empty maple fingers stand
like stripes across the sky.
Parading clouds shadow the land;
in darkness, they float by.

Orange pumpkins, yellow gourds,
grow plumply in green patches
and soon will bring harvest rewards
as we bake pies in batches.
One hundred and ten days, at least,
a pumpkin needs to grow,
and patience brings us to our feast
when time ticks on too slow.
The goo is emptied from gourd skin,
his salty seeds are fried,
his smile comes to bright life
as a candle's put inside.

There are some times, as winter nears
and skies are turning gray,
we need a friend to ease our fears
and tell us it's okay.
The earth's the same in this respect
by harvest number three;
she grows a tough skin to protect
late fruits from early freeze.
Needing some help is never wrong,
it comes as we adjust.
In fact, it means your mind is strong,
and in yourself, you trust.

The sunlight falls out of the day
the harvest moon does rise,
and smoky clouds float, dark and gray,
across the ashen skies.
The voices we have missed will call
upon our ears, tonight.
They whisper as the brown leaves fall
to tell us it's alright.
They thank us for our paid respect,
for all the candles burned,
and over us they will protect
until they next return.

Special plates for special meals
like this, our Samhain feast.
Our oven fire is ablaze
and smells of rising yeast.
For fresh bread, veggies, fruit, and pies,
we gather at the table
then open up our ears and eyes
to hear a Samhain fable.
One of our chairs remains empty,
in honor of a friend;
it warms our hearts and minds to see
her memory will not end.

*Under a moon so full and bright,
may you sleep peacefully tonight.*

MY FAMILY TRADITIONS

Every family has its own special traditions that make holidays truly magickal.
Use this space to write or draw about some of your favorite holiday fun.

YULE:

IMBOLGC:

OSTARA:

BELTANE:

MIDSUMMER:

LAMMAS:

MABON:

SAMHAIN:

ABOUT THE AUTHOR

J.C. Artemisia is a communications professor with a master's degree in education and a bachelor's degree in creative writing. She is a pantheist Pagan and the proud mother to three, happy children. In addition to writing and visual art, she enjoys reading, crocheting, and baking up some kitchen magick. You can follow her updates and musings at www.facebook.com/JCArtemisiaBooks.

Made in the USA
Lexington, KY
31 December 2017